"This photo of me and my buddies was taken around April 1969 in the A Shau Valley in South Vietnam," Private Mike Serrato remembered 40 years later. "We had just come in from a reconnaissance mission. I am in the middle. Chuck Paige 'Preacher' from L.A. was on my right, and Randy, or 'Beatle'—I think from Missouri—was on my left."

A month later, the three men would take part in one of the bloodiest battles of the Vietnam War.

U.S. soldiers keep low as they rush a wounded comrade to a medical aid station during the Battle of Hamburger Hill.

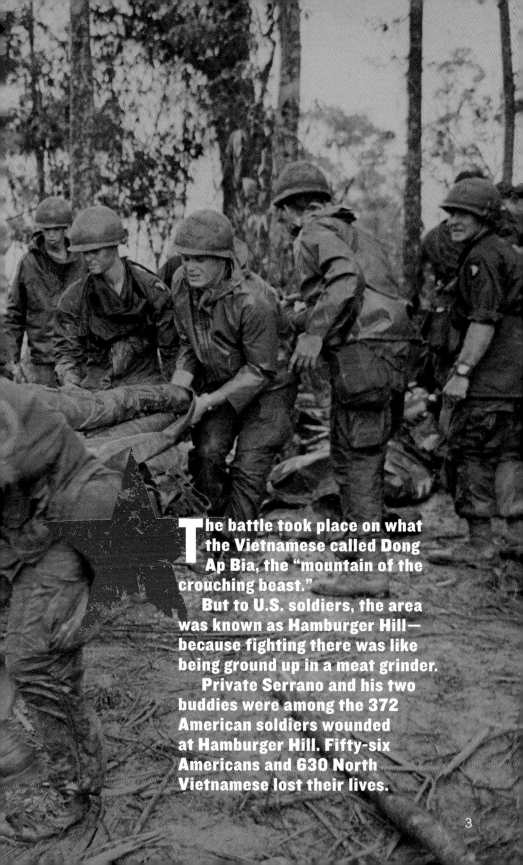

The battle took place on what the Vietnamese called Dong Ap Bia, the "mountain of the crouching beast."

But to U.S. soldiers, the area was known as Hamburger Hill—because fighting there was like being ground up in a meat grinder.

Private Serrano and his two buddies were among the 372 American soldiers wounded at Hamburger Hill. Fifty-six Americans and 630 North Vietnamese lost their lives.

Photographs © 2010: **AP Images:** 18 bottom (Horst Faas), 28, 29 (Art Greenspon), back cover, 5, 12 bottom, 13 bottom, 21, 22 bottom, 23, 38 top, 47, 56 top; **From the personal collection of Arthur Wiknik Jr.:** 33 top, 44, 45, 48, 50, 55 bottom; **Corbis Images:** 2, 3, 14, 15, 25, 27, 34, 42, 43, 51 (Shunsuke Akatsuka/Bettmann), cover (Shunsuke Akatsuka/Bettmann, hand-tinted by Red Herring Design), 7 top, 37 top, 46 (Nathan Benn), 9 top, 17, 31 bottom, 33 bottom, 33 center, 39 bottom, 40, 41 bottom, 53 (Bettmann), 35 (Tim Page), 20; **From the personal collection of Frank Boccia:** 16 bottom, 16 top, 54 bottom; **Getty Images:** 37 bottom (AFP), 8, 11 top (Larry Burrows/Time Life Pictures), 8 right, 9 left (Hulton Archive), 57 (Will & Deni McIntyre); **From the personal collection of John Snyder:** 26; **La Porte County Historical Society Museum:** 32 bottom; **Magnum/Philip Jones Griffiths:** 7 bottom; **From the personal collection of Michael Serrano:** 1, 30, 31 top, 54 top, 55 top; **National Archives and Records Administration:** 18 top (U.S. Air Force), 56 (U.S. Information Agency), 36, 41 top (U.S. Marine Corps); **OnAsia/Mai Nam:** 11 bottom; **Stockphoto.com/Black Star:** 32 top (Vernon Merritt), 52 (Jim Pickerell); **The Granger Collection, New York:** 10 (Jacoby/ullstein bild), 24; **U.S. Army Photo/ Fort Campbell MWR:** 49; **VietnamGear.com:** 22 top, 38 bottom, 39 top; **Woodfin Camp & Associates/Alan Copeland:** 13 top.

Maps by David Lindroth, Inc.

CONTENT CONSULTANT: David L. Anderson, Ph.D., Professor of History, Division of Social, Behavioral, and Global Studies, California State University, Monterey Bay

Book design: Red Herring Design/NYC

Library of Congress Cataloging-in-Publication Data
DiConsiglio, John.
Vietnam : the bloodbath at Hamburger Hill / John DiConsiglio.
p. cm. — (24/7 goes to war)
Includes bibliographical references and index.
ISBN-13: 978-0-531-25526-1 (lib. bdg.) 978-0-531-25451-6 (pbk.)
ISBN-10: 0-531-25526-3 (lib. bdg.) 0-531-25451-8 (pbk.)
1. Hamburger Hill, Battle of, Vietnam, 1969—Juvenile literature.
I. Title.
DS557.8.A54D53 2010
959.704'342—dc22 2009014912

VIETNAM

The Bloodbath at Hamburger Hill

JOHN DiCONSIGLIO

Franklin Watts®
An Imprint of Scholastic Inc.

CHINA

NORTH VIETNAM
(Democratic Republic
of Vietnam)

Hanoi

NORTH

WEST ● EAST

SOUTH

Gulf of Tonkin

L A O S

Mekong River

T H A I L A N D

DMZ

Khe Sanh

Hue

Da Nang
China Beach

HAMBURGER HILL

May 10–20, 1969

Hamburger Hill is a small mountain in the
A Shau Valley in South Vietnam. It was the
site of ten days of intense fighting.

Gulf of
Thailand

C A M B O D I A

SOUTH
VIETNAM
(Republic of
Vietnam)

Saigon

MEKONG
DELTA

South
China Sea

KEY

North Vietnam

South Vietnam

DMZ
(demilitarized zone)

national capital

0   100 mi.

0   100 km

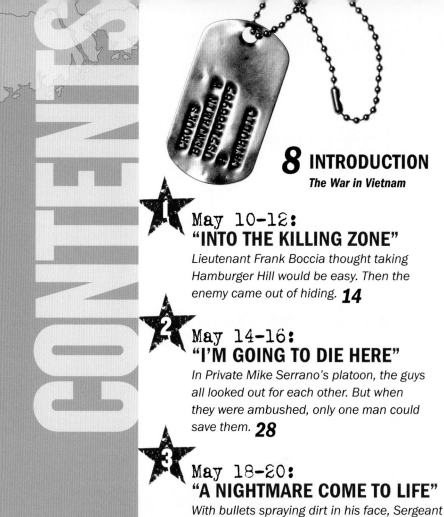

CONTENTS

8 **INTRODUCTION**
The War in Vietnam

★ **1**

May 10-12:
"INTO THE KILLING ZONE"
Lieutenant Frank Boccia thought taking Hamburger Hill would be easy. Then the enemy came out of hiding. **14**

★ **2**

May 14-16:
"I'M GOING TO DIE HERE"
In Private Mike Serrano's platoon, the guys all looked out for each other. But when they were ambushed, only one man could save them. **28**

★ **3**

May 18-20:
"A NIGHTMARE COME TO LIFE"
With bullets spraying dirt in his face, Sergeant Arthur Wiknik was sure he was about to die. That's when he did something crazy. **42**

54 **POSTSCRIPT**
Home from the War

56 **AFTERWORD**
War Wounds

58 *TIMELINE*
59 *RESOURCES*
60 *DICTIONARY*
62 *INDEX*
64 *ABOUT THIS BOOK*

THE WAR IN VIETNAM

U.S. Marines land on
the beach at Da Nang,
Vietnam, in 1965 (above).
A U.S. soldier on patrol in
1966 (right).

The heat is like a furnace. One hundred degrees. Probably more. Even the driving rain doesn't cool you off. Your combat boots sink deep in the mud as you shuffle through the jungle. You grip your rifle. The enemy could be anywhere. Maybe behind that thicket of trees. Or dug deep in a spider hole. Always ready to attack.

Your stomach growls. You haven't bathed in a week. And you can't remember the last time you slept.

It's 1969. You're an American teenager. And you're a soldier in South Vietnam.

Draftees being inducted into the army in 1968

U.S. combat troops served in Vietnam from 1965 to 1975. It was the longest and most controversial war in U.S. history, and it was fought mostly by kids just out of high school. They were shipped across the world, to a nation in Southeast Asia. And as the years went by and the body count mounted, Americans wondered: How did U.S. soldiers ever end up in Vietnam?

Vietnam Split in Two

The answer goes back at least as far as 1954, when Vietnam was split into two parts—North and South Vietnam. The leader of North Vietnam, Ho Chi Minh, proclaimed the country communist. That's a system in which one all-powerful party controls its citizens' economic and political lives.

The leader of South Vietnam, Ngo Dinh Diem, was opposed to communism.

That conflict would lead to war.

9

At the time, communism was a growing force around the world. It had taken root in the Soviet Union and China, and was now spreading into Southeast Asia. As the world's leading democracy, the United States opposed communism. It vowed to help any country threatened by a communist takeover.

South Vietnam's leader, Ngo Dinh Diem, feared that his country faced exactly that threat. Ho Chi Minh had made it clear that he planned to take over South Vietnam. He wanted to make it part of a united, all-communist Vietnam.

With Ho Chi Minh's support, communist rebels in South Vietnam—the Viet Cong—were launching raids and conducting assassinations throughout South Vietnam.

A U.S. military adviser trains South Vietnamese villagers in 1962.

To help South Vietnam, the U.S. government began sending military advisers and economic aid. It feared that if South Vietnam fell to the communists, neighboring countries such as Laos, Cambodia, and Thailand would topple like "dominoes."

In 1964, U.S. President Lyndon Johnson asked Congress to give him the power to "take all necessary steps, including the use of armed forces" to help South Vietnam. By 1967, 400,000 U.S. troops were fighting in Vietnam. American air strikes targeted enemy positions in North and South Vietnam.

Viet Cong rebels operate a machine gun in Ha Tinh province, 1967.

A U.S. air strike against Viet Cong rebels in a South Vietnamese village

Bogged Down

But the enemy showed no signs of weakening. And American troops had to fight both a regular army—the North Vietnamese Army (NVA)—and the Viet Cong rebels. The Viet Cong used guerrilla tactics such as hiding in the jungle, waiting to ambush U.S. patrols. Then they would escape through intricate networks of underground tunnels.

Soon, U.S. troops—known as GIs—were bogged down in a treacherous jungle war. Often, they couldn't tell who was friendly and who was the enemy. Many Viet Cong fighters were women dressed in civilian clothes; sometimes even children fought.

"The worst nightmare I ever had about Vietnam was that I had to go back," says filmmaker Oliver Stone, who served in the war.

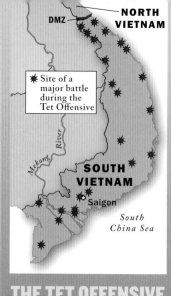

Site of a major battle during the Tet Offensive

DMZ

NORTH VIETNAM

Mekong River

SOUTH VIETNAM

Saigon

South China Sea

THE TET OFFENSIVE
During the Tet Offensive, the North hit more than 100 targets in South Vietnam.

By early 1967, U.S. deaths topped 8,000. Soldiers suffered from low morale. At home, only half the country supported the war.

In January 1968, the North Vietnamese launched a surprise attack. They targeted cities and military bases throughout South Vietnam. Known as the Tet Offensive, the massive assault was a military failure for the North. But it made Americans realize that the enemy was still highly organized and determined. The war probably wouldn't end soon, and casualties were continuing to mount. By the end of 1968, 36,000 U.S. troops had lost their lives.

"A Feeling of Doom"

A vigorous anti-war movement gripped the nation. In November 1969, 500,000 protesters marched in Washington, D.C., demanding an end to the war.

But the war continued. One of the bloodiest battles would take place in the A Shau Valley, in South Vietnam. After Tet, units of the

NVA had retreated to the valley to rebuild their base, train new soldiers, and stockpile weapons. Determined to destroy those units, the U.S. Army launched "Operation Apache Snow."

In May 1969, as part of the operation, U.S. troops were ordered to take Hill 937—a military name for the hill's height in meters, the equivalent of about 3,000 feet.

It seemed like a simple assault. But the NVA had turned the hill into a giant deathtrap. Heavily armed soldiers hid in deep tunnels. Snipers in trees waited to pick off the invaders. "There was a feeling of evil there. A feeling of doom," says Mike Serrano, a soldier who fought on what came to be called Hamburger Hill.

The ten-day battle was brutal—one of the bloodiest of the Vietnam War. On the following pages, you'll read the personal accounts of three soldiers who fought there.

Two U.S. soldiers take cover in high grass during a battle in 1967. One of them (above) carries a radio on his back.

1

May 10-12:
"INTO THE M

Medics help soldiers injured
during the fighting on
Hamburger Hill.

LLING ZONE"

Lieutenant Frank Boccia thought taking Hamburger Hill would be easy. Then the enemy came out of hiding.

FRANK BOCCIA

Frank Boccia, age 16, in Italy with relatives

HOMETOWN:
Washington, D.C.

GRADUATED COLLEGE:
1966

AGE WHEN HE ENLISTED:
23

RANK:
Lieutenant

UNIT:
3rd Battalion, 187th Regiment, 101st Airborne

ARRIVED IN VIETNAM:
December 1968

As a kid growing up in Washington, D.C., Frank Boccia believed he lived in the greatest country on earth.

Boccia had a privileged childhood. His father was a diplomat, and the family enjoyed first-class trips to Europe and dinner parties with powerful people.

When Boccia graduated from college, he thought about studying English literature. Instead, he did something totally unexpected. He joined the U.S. Army.

"If you took a poll of my classmates in high school, I would have been the last person they'd pick to be in the army," Boccia recalls. "I was short—5'7". Maybe 145 pounds. I was shy. I had illusions of being an intellectual, not a soldier. But I owed this country my service."

It was 1968 and the Vietnam War was raging. Boccia had just gotten married. His wife was pregnant with their first child.

A lieutenant, Boccia served with the 3rd Battalion of the 187th Regiment, 101st Airborne Division—or, in army shorthand, the 3/187th. The 3/187th had a reputation as the bravest fighters who took on the toughest jobs. Under the command of the hard-nosed Lieutenant Colonel Weldon Honeycutt, they were about to receive their toughest assignment ever.

As Boccia explains, it was their job to lead the assault on Hill 937—Hamburger Hill.

Boccia during the Battle of Hamburger Hill

May 10: The Battle Begins

I had been in Vietnam for a few months [before Hamburger Hill]. I was a fairly popular platoon leader. Sure, I was strict and demanding. But I made an effort to know all my guys by name. I'd ask them about their families. I wanted them to know I cared about them. We were a tight platoon.

Lieutenant Colonel Weldon Honeycutt was a different breed of cat. He was tough and abrasive. He had these ice-blue eyes that looked at you like he might just cut your throat. No one liked him. But he was the best combat commander I've ever seen.

His code name was Blackjack. He told me that the only reason the army made me an officer was because I was too educated to do anything else. He said I had a lot to learn about leading men and making tough choices in battle. I was furious at him. He made me feel about an inch tall.

NVA soldiers run along a barbed-wire fence during a training exercise in 1967.

My battalion, the 3/187th, went into the A Shau Valley on May 10. The A Shau had a terrible reputation as a dangerous hideout for the North Vietnamese Army (NVA). None of us talked about it, though. It was like the elephant in the room. Still, we weren't strangers to combat. We'd been in a hard firefight at another mountain called Dong Ngai. After that fight, I expected this one to be easy.

The sky above the valley was filled with helicopters—Hueys, as they were known. As my platoon prepared to move up the hill, it seemed like every helicopter in Vietnam circled over us. I'd read accounts of D-Day in World War II and how soldiers were awestruck by the sight of all the ships assembled around them.

That's how I felt. There were hundreds of soldiers in the valley. I got goose bumps. I thought, "Is the entire army here?"

Napalm bombs explode on a Viet Cong position in 1965.

Before my platoon moved up the hill, fighter-bombers and artillery helicopters bombarded its slopes with air strikes and napalm [gasoline-based firebombs]. It didn't seem like anything could be alive up there.

But as we approached the mountain, I could tell this mission would be more difficult than I anticipated. Each step was a struggle. Narrow trails snaked up

U.S. helicopters support South Vietnamese troops during an attack on a Viet Cong camp.

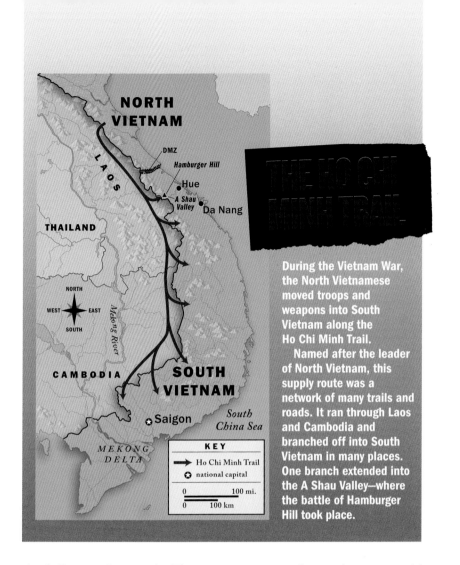

THE HO CHI MINH TRAIL

During the Vietnam War, the North Vietnamese moved troops and weapons into South Vietnam along the Ho Chi Minh Trail.

Named after the leader of North Vietnam, this supply route was a network of many trails and roads. It ran through Laos and Cambodia and branched off into South Vietnam in many places. One branch extended into the A Shau Valley—where the battle of Hamburger Hill took place.

KEY

→ Ho Chi Minh Trail
✪ national capital

0   100 mi.
0   100 km

the hill into the jungle. The canopy was so dense that we could barely see a few feet ahead of us. The vines kept out the light and the fresh air. The jungle smelled rotten. It gave me a feeling of being completely out of the world.

Suddenly we heard shots over our heads. An intense blast of RPGs [rocket-propelled grenades] and AK-47 gunfire cut through the trees. I couldn't see where it was coming from— bushes, vines, or rocks.

We hit the ground and returned fire. But the skirmish was brief. The enemy was gone as mysteriously as they'd arrived.

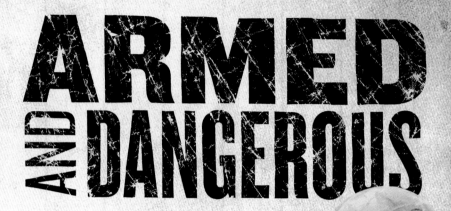

ARMED
AND DANGEROUS

U.S. AND SOUTH VIETNAM

MARK 2 GRENADES
A GI could throw one of these grenades 30 yards. An explosive inside the grenade would shatter the casing, sending small metal fragments, or shrapnel, flying. A Mark 2 was deadly within 15 yards of where it landed.

M-79 GRENADE LAUNCHER
Known as the "Thumper," the M-79 looked like a sawed-off shotgun. It could accurately fire grenades, smoke bombs, and flares to nearly 700 feet.

M-60 MACHINE GUN
This lightweight weapon was easier to carry on patrols than older machine guns, but like those, it took two men to operate—a gunner and his assistant. The gun was fired from tripods or attached to tanks or helicopters. It had a range of 1,900 yards and a maximum firing rate of 550 rounds per minute.

M-16 RIFLE
Most U.S. troops carried short, light M-16s. In the early years of the war, the gun jammed easily and was hard to keep clean in the field. An improved version was later developed. The M-16's bullets were held in metal clips, or magazines, that popped into the rifle.

In the dense jungles of Vietnam, firefights often erupted without warning. To survive, troops had to react quickly. That meant they needed lightweight weapons that were reliable—and deadly. Here's a look at some of the weapons used during the war.

VIET CONG AND NORTH VIETNAM

AK-47 ASSAULT RIFLE

Also known as the "Kalashnikov." Heavier and less accurate than the M-16, this gun's solid frame made it more durable in the jungle.

RPG-2 ROCKET LAUNCHER

This lightweight, shoulder-held weapon fired a rocket-propelled grenade (RPG) that exploded on impact. It was used against armored vehicles, enemy fortifications, and helicopters. The RPG-2 was eventually replaced by the more accurate RPG-7.

81-MM MORTAR

This short, portable cannon could shoot a 15-inch rocket the length of a football field. It took a three-man crew to carry the bulky weapon.

May 11: Ambushed

In the morning, we marched up the trail again.

An NVA soldier's canteen

We hadn't gone far before we found the bodies of three dead NVA soldiers. Lying nearby were two rifles, an RPG launcher, and six grenades.

One of the dead men had a picture of a woman and a letter sticking out of his pocket. I guess he was writing home to his wife. I didn't feel bad for him. He was a soldier like us. We all knew what we were getting into. But I was sad for his family. I couldn't help thinking about my own wife and unborn child back home.

As we moved forward, we found more signs of the NVA— bandages, footprints, rucksacks filled with rice balls. One of my privates turned to me. "Something's wrong here, Lieutenant," he said.

He was right. The NVA were usually careful about hiding their tracks. Why were they being this clumsy? "It's like they're laying out a road map for us," the private said. They were luring us into a trap.

The trail was narrow and steep, lined with bamboo trees as thick as steel walls. We walked in single file, like a long freight train. My platoon was

A GI rushes for cover from sniper fire in 1967.

200 meters [650 feet] behind the leaders. I couldn't see anything. But I heard bursts of gunfire ahead. The lead platoon had walked into a clearing—and straight into an ambush. It was chaos. I was stuck in that single-file line as bloodied men limped back down the trail. I still wasn't sure what happened even as we pulled back.

But it was now clear that we were in for a fight. Our scouts

translated documents found on the dead NVA soldiers. We learned that hundreds of NVA were dug into the hill. They were everywhere—burrowed deep into spider holes and tunnels, tied to the jungle treetops.

Worse, the soldiers were part of the 29th NVA Regiment—an elite fighting force. The Vietnamese dubbed them the "Pride of Ho Chi Minh." They had a well-deserved reputation as "American Killers."

May 12: Into the Killing Zone

Honeycutt sent us back up the hill on the 12th.

This time, my platoon took the lead on that narrow trail—into the Killing Zone, as we called the clearing. At first we saw nothing. Then an NVA soldier popped out of a bunker and fired an RPG. The enemy always aimed their rocket grenades at the trees above us. When the grenade exploded, it showered us in sharp metal and wood shards.

The first RPG shot was a signal. Suddenly, countless NVA soldiers appeared from spider holes, firing volleys of RPGs. We hugged the ground, but grenade rockets kept coming. About 30 NVA soldiers laid down a blanket of machine-gun fire. Tree limbs and branches fell around us. We tried to shoot back, but the assault was too intense. I couldn't even lift my head.

U.S. soldiers pull a Viet Cong fighter from his hiding place in a spider hole—a small, camouflaged pit in the ground.

An enemy rocket explodes behind a U.S. soldier during the assault on Hamburger Hill. The soldier was seriously wounded.

I radioed my captain. "We're in a firefight," I shouted. "It's unbelievably heavy. I've never seen anything like this. If we stay here we're going to get chopped up."

He ordered us to retreat down the hill. I yelled for my men to pull back. But then a cold feeling hit the pit of my stomach. One man would have to stay behind. Someone had to lay down cover fire to keep the NVA from slaughtering us as we retreated.

I looked at the Killing Zone. Specialist John Snyder was pinned behind a log. He was nearest to the enemy. It would

Specialist John Snyder in Vietnam, holding an M-60 machine gun

Soldiers wounded during the fighting on May 12 wait for MedEvac helicopters to airlift them from Hamburger Hill to a nearby base hospital.

have to be him. I gave the order. I was essentially condemning John to death. But it was the only way to get the rest of us out safely. It was a wrenching decision. At that moment I realized what Honeycutt had been trying to tell me. Being an officer isn't fun and games. It's an awesome responsibility.

John should have died. But he was lucky. A grenade hit his helmet. It bounced in the air and exploded behind him. He made a wild lunge to safety. It was a small victory. But as we rolled back down that hill, gunfire following behind us, I thought, "My God, what have we gotten into?"

2

May 14-16: "I'M GOING TO

During the Vietnam War, MedEvac helicopters flew into battle zones to pick up wounded soldiers. Here, soldiers in a jungle clearing near Hue, South Vietnam, wait to be evacuated.

DIE HERE"

In Private Mike Serrano's platoon, the guys all looked out for each other. But when they were ambushed, only one man could save them.

MIKE SERRANO

HOMETOWN:
San Leandro, CA

GRADUATED HIGH SCHOOL:
1966

AGE WHEN DRAFTED:
19

RANK:
Private

UNIT:
1st Battalion, 506th Regiment, 101st Airborne

ARRIVED IN VIETNAM:
November 1968

When Mike Serrano graduated from high school in 1966, he knew that his next stop would be Vietnam.

Several of Serrano's friends had already been drafted into the army. They'd received the government form letter that ordered them to report for duty.

Serrano's draft letter showed up in his mailbox in March 1968. He didn't know what to expect when he got to Vietnam. His friends who'd returned from the war didn't want to talk about it.

Still, at 19, Serrano wasn't scared of going to war. To him, it was as much a part of growing up as getting his driver's license. His father and uncles had fought in World War II. "I felt it was my turn now," he recalls. "It was like some big John Wayne adventure."

Serrano became a private with the 1st Battalion of the 506th Infantry Regiment—the 1/506th. On May 13, 1969, his battalion arrived on Hamburger Hill to reinforce Frank Boccia's unit. But as Serrano recalls, things didn't work out as planned.

Mike Serrano in South Vietnam in February 1969. His commander wanted his soldiers clean-shaven so the enemy would think "we were fresh troops," Serrano recalled.

Spring 1969: In an Eerie Place

During a mission in February 1969, Serrano took time out to pose with two Vietnamese kids.

In May 1969, I was on a three-day [leave] at Vietnam's China Beach. It was a coastal resort on the South China Sea where American soldiers went to surf and take a break from the war. I was hanging out with an old high-school buddy. I had such a good time that I almost missed the helicopter back to my unit.

When I returned to the 1/506th, my friend Chuck Page said he was sorry to see me. He was hoping I'd miss that chopper.

A U.S. platoon on patrol in the A Shau Valley in 1968

We were going on a mission, he said. And it didn't sound good. The 3/187th [Frank Boccia's unit] was engaged in a fierce fight with a strong NVA force on Hill 937. We were supposed to be their reinforcements.

My battalion had patrolled the A Shau Valley since early spring. It was a place of malevolent beauty. Some of it was lush and green and as pretty as a postcard. But there was also this eerie feeling in the valley. We had a Vietnamese scout who was terrified by it. "Very bad," he warned us. "*Beaucoup* [lots of] killers." He ran away rather than go into that valley.

But soldiers don't think about the dangers—or at least they don't talk about it. Soldiers adapted to the Vietnam jungles. You had to if you wanted to survive.

You got very little sleep. It was horribly hot; you were always

In a rare moment of peace, a soldier reads a letter from home.

dripping with sweat. Most of the time you ate out of cans. When you were in the field, you were lucky if you took a shower once a month. You were more concerned about keeping your socks dry than about the enemy.

It didn't take long for us to figure out that all we really wanted was for us and our buddies to be safe.

May 14–15:
An Invisible Enemy

We were led by Sergeant Roger Pedue.

Roger stuck out in our camp. The platoon was mostly 18-year-old kids from big cities like New York and Los Angeles. Roger was a lanky blond farm boy from Indiana. At 26, he was an old man to us. We teased him for being a "lifer"—a career military man among

Roger Pedue, pictured in his hometown newspaper

Greeting: You are hereby ordered for induction into the armed forces of the United States.

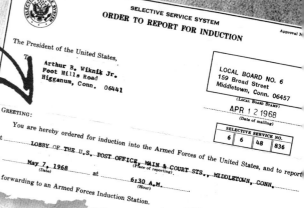

SELECTIVE SERVICE SYSTEM
ORDER TO REPORT FOR INDUCTION

The President of the United States,

To
Arthur B. Wiknik Jr.
Foot Hills Road
Higganum, Conn. 06441

LOCAL BOARD NO. 6
159 Broad Street
Middletown, Conn. 06457

GREETING:

You are hereby ordered for induction into the Armed Forces of the United States, and to report

at LOBBY OF THE U.S. POST OFFICE, MAIN & COURT STS., MIDDLETOWN, CONN.

on May 7, 1968 at 6:30 A.M.

for forwarding to an Armed Forces Induction Station.

Those were the first words in the draft notice that millions of young American men received during the Vietnam War. If you received this letter, it meant you had to join the U.S. military.

Millions of young men received a draft notice from the U.S. president.

DRAFTED

During the war, the U.S. government used a system called the draft to fill the ranks of the armed services.

If a male citizen was between the ages of 18 and 26, he had to register for the draft. Shortly after his eighteenth birthday, he was required to register his name, address, and other details with the government. Then he would receive a draft card, which was proof that he had registered.

Early in the war, local draft boards decided who had to serve. But people complained that the system was unfair—it gave the people on draft boards too much power. The government switched to a national lottery, which selected draftees at random.

Draftees in 1968. About 30 percent of U.S. troops in Vietnam were drafted.

As the war dragged on, opposition to the draft grew. Some draft resisters burned their draft cards at anti-war rallies. Tens of thousands broke the law by refusing to serve. To avoid going to jail, many of them moved to Canada.

A few years after the war ended, President Jimmy Carter pardoned 10,000 so-called "draft dodgers," allowing them to come home.

During a 1967 protest, a man burns his draft card.

draftees. All he ever wanted to be was a soldier. But we trusted Roger with our lives. He was like a mother hen, making sure we were safe.

On May 14, we started up the hill. We heard gunfire and air strikes. The battle was well underway.

We weren't a quarter of the way to the summit before we were attacked. I didn't even see the enemy. They jumped out of these deeply dug bunkers and fired at us from every angle. The noise was deafening.

The fighting was so bad that helicopters couldn't land to resupply our ammo. They hovered overhead and kicked guns down to us on the ground.

We fought all day on the 14th. On the 15th, we got a little higher up the hill—maybe a third of the way up. But we took heavy casualties from NVA ambushes. They weren't going to let

A group of U.S. soldiers advance up Hamburger Hill during the battle.

us up that hill—no ifs, ands, or buts. We clawed for every inch of ground.

We set up camp on the night of the 15th. I heard tree branches rustling in the dark. The NVA were moving around us, digging in for the morning attacks.

Our radio operator had been killed, and I was picked to take his place. I wasn't sure if I wanted to. Everyone knew the enemy aimed for the guy with the radio on his back. I'd be an easy target.

But the radio guy also got first pick of candy and cigarettes. I decided it was worth it.

Radio operators kept platoon leaders in touch with their commanders.

May 16: As Good as Dead

At dawn, Roger walked by as I was strapping on the radio.

At first, he didn't say anything. He reached into his pocket and pulled out a pack of cigarettes. He lit one and handed the rest to me. Then he calmly told me that our platoon would lead the attack.

There was silence between us. Roger looked me in the eyes. "You know, they're waiting for us, Mike," he said. I nodded. The NVA were planning an ambush. The point man in our unit—the soldier in the lead—would be as good as dead.

Roger blew smoke into the air. Our squad was a bunch of guys who hadn't been in Nam long. There were only two men experienced enough to walk point, Roger said. "Me and you."

A U.S. Marine walks point for his unit during a mission in Vietnam in 1966.

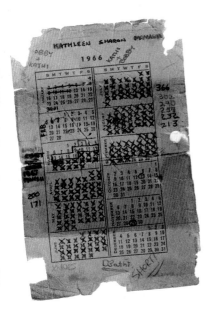

A GI's calendar shows the days he's served in Vietnam. On the upper right, he has recorded the number of days he has left.

He stomped his cigarette under his boot and gave me a cockeyed grin. "And I'm better at it than you," he smiled. "Besides, we can't afford to lose the radio."

I realized what he was saying. Roger knew he was going to die.

Roger rarely talked about himself. But as we stood there, he told me about a girl back in Indiana. He was in love with her. She had two children, and he cared for them like they were his own. "If I ever get out of this, Mike," he said, "I'm gonna ask that girl to marry me."

It was almost time for the company to move out. Roger told me to take care of the men. My heart was racing. He was saying good-bye.

I could have volunteered to walk point. But the words wouldn't come out. I just said, "Roger, don't be a hero."

He smiled and walked away.

Saving His Men

A few minutes later, we started up the hill.

Roger was on point. We were no more than 150 feet out when Roger stopped in the trail. Suddenly, he sprayed gunfire into the trees. That's when all hell broke loose.

It was an ambush. Roger must have seen something. Rather than have us walk into a shooting gallery, he sprung the trap.

Viet Cong fighters hide in a field of lotus flowers, waiting for the enemy.

37

A paratrooper from the 101st Division tries to save a fellow soldier's life by performing mouth-to-mouth resuscitation.

NVA soldiers popped out of spider holes. They dropped from trees. Roger was hit first. He rolled off the trail.

He could have laid there quietly until a medic got to him. Instead, he tossed grenades at the enemy. The NVA aimed all of their firepower at him. That gave the rest of us time to move into position. But Roger was struck with round after round. He never had a chance.

I crawled to one side of the trail and tried to work the radio. It was busted. Then my M-16 rifle jammed. I was a sitting duck.

A rocket grenade exploded next to me. Shrapnel—sharp metal fragments—pierced my right arm

A U.S. military M79 grenade vest. It could hold up to 24 rounds.

and leg. My left foot was bleeding bad. I could feel my right side going numb when my friend Chuck somehow found me. He yelled at me to hold on for a medic. Then he looked at my back.

"Oh my god, Mike," he gasped. A hail of shrapnel had ripped the radio on my back apart—but it stopped the shrapnel. That radio saved my life.

"It Could Have Been Me"
I barely remember being carried off the hill.

Someone dragged me back to the perimeter with the wounded and the dead. A medic screamed that a MedEvac chopper was on its way.

The guy lying next to me had half his leg shot off. I could see the bone protruding from his knee. I heard constant gunfire from the hill.

This military radio had a range of five miles.

That's when it started raining. Waves of water fell over me in sheets, washing the blood down my arms and legs. I was soaking wet and shivering. I remember thinking, *I'm never getting off this hill. I'm going to die here.*

I looked over at a row of dead bodies in the clearing. They were covered in plastic ponchos. The rain beat down on them. The wind blew a poncho aside and I saw a soldier's bloody leg. Someone told me it was Roger.

A wounded soldier talks to a chaplain as he waits to be airlifted off Hamburger Hill.

Soldiers rush a wounded American soldier to a MedEvac helicopter that has just landed on Hamburger Hill.

I sat there in the rain looking at Roger. I could hear the MedEvac chopper blades coming closer. The medic yelled at me to hold on. I stared at Roger's body. It could have been me under that poncho.

I shook my head. Why did Roger die? Why did I live?

Two marines try to find shelter from the rain in January 1969.

3

May 18-20: "A NIGHT

On May 18, soldiers arrived
by helicopter to reinforce U.S.
troops on Hamburger Hill.

With bullets spraying dirt in his face, Sergeant Arthur Wiknik was sure he was about to die. That's when he did something crazy.

MARE COME TO LIFE"

ARTHUR WIKNIK

HOMETOWN:
Higganum, CT

GRADUATED HIGH SCHOOL:
1966

AGE WHEN DRAFTED: 19

RANK:
Sergeant

UNIT:
2nd Battalion, 506th Regiment, 101st Airborne

ARRIVED IN VIETNAM:
April 1969

He had the world at his fingertips. Arthur Wiknik was a 19-year-old with a new Chevrolet Camaro, a steady girlfriend, and a good job.

"I was having the time of my life," Wiknik recalls. "And then, well, everything changed."

It was 1968—and Wiknik was drafted. He was on his way to Vietnam. And he didn't want to go. "It's not that I was a coward. But I wasn't a hero either," he says.

A self-proclaimed joker, Wiknik wanted no part of combat. When asked on an army document what job he was qualified for, Wiknik wrote, "chaplain's assistant." His second choice was "pastry chef."

Instead, the army trained Wiknik to become a sergeant. He was assigned to the 2nd Battalion of the 506th Infantry Regiment—the 2/506th.

Wiknik arrived in Vietnam in April 1969, never having been in combat. He wondered how he would react when the bullets started flying. Could he keep his head and lead men into battle?

"I guess I was looking for a chance to prove myself," he says.

Less than a month later, Wiknik got his chance—on Hamburger Hill.

Arthur Wiknik
in Da Nang,
South Vietnam,
in 1970

May 18: Heading Into Battle

I was only in Vietnam for three weeks before our entire company—about 120 men—got a vacation.

We went to Eagle Beach, a rest stop in central Vietnam near the Huong River. It was a giant picnic. We stuffed ourselves on hot dogs, hamburgers, and beer. We went waterskiing and swimming. I started to think maybe the army wasn't going to be that bad after all.

But three days later, our captain gathered us together. The picnic was over. "Men," he said, "we're going into the A Shau Valley. Some of our buddies have run into trouble out there. And we're going to help."

On May 18, we piled into helicopters. Six men to a bird, our feet dangling out the doors. They loaded us down with ammunition. We usually carried 200 rounds of ammo. This time we brought 400. Instead of two grenades each, we all had four.

We were heading into something big.

We flew over the valley. The hills were pockmarked from bombs. I could make out Hill 937 from the air. It was a brown patch in the middle of a green backdrop. Right away, I knew that's where the action was. For the last eight days, the hill had been torn apart by bombs, napalm, air strikes, mortars, you name it. There was nothing left but mud and slop and trees that looked like twisted telephone poles.

We hovered over the LZ [landing zone], about a half mile from the mountain. Our pilot screamed over the roar of the rotors, "It's too risky to land!" NVA troops were firing at the helicopters. We'd have to jump.

The door gunner blasted his M-60 machine gun into the jungle, and one by one my men jumped into the matted valley grass. I didn't want to go. I had 60 pounds of gear on my back. Gunfire was coming from everywhere.

I yelled at the pilot to land that bird. I wasn't jumping!

Then the door gunner kicked me in the back. He pushed me off the helicopter. I fell ten feet to the ground—and landed right on my face.

As I dusted myself off, I looked around the valley. There must have been 300 other GIs there. [More than 1,000 GIs fought in the ten-day battle.] We spent the day digging in and re-building damaged bunkers. At night, the NVA crawled out of their tunnels and lit fires. Our guys shelled the side of the hill just to let them know we were still there.

U.S. soldiers wear an ID plate called a dog tag

May 19: "They Looked Like Zombies"
On the 19th, my company moved into position.

As we walked the narrow ridge trails along the base of the hill, we could see the remnants of the battle. It was like a nightmare come to life.

The trail was littered with discarded equipment—half-used machine-gun belts, M-16 ammunition magazines, empty cans, canteens, ponchos. We also saw body bags on the trail's edge, each with a dead American inside. I remember thinking, "What happened here?"

All the grass was trampled into the dirt. There was garbage

THE HELICOPTER WAR

Helicopters played a huge role in the Vietnam War. The two most commonly used helicopters were the UH-1 Huey and the CH-47 Chinook. They were used for a variety of purposes.

TROOP TRANSPORT

Transport helicopters airlifted troops in and out of hard-to-reach places in the jungle. During a major battle, hundreds of choppers—each carrying up to 32 soldiers—could be called into action. "Door gunners" firing machine guns from the helicopters' open doors provided some protection from enemy fire.

AIRBORNE ASSAULT

Armor-plated gunships known as "Cobras" or "Hogs" supported ground troops by attacking enemy positions from the air. They were equipped with machine guns, grenade launchers, and rocket launchers.

MEDICAL EVACUATION

MedEvac "air ambulances" airlifted wounded soldiers to hospitals at nearby military bases. Some soldiers received treatment within 30 minutes of being injured. Mostly because of MedEvacs, 81% of soldiers wounded in Vietnam survived, compared to 71% in World War II.

SEARCH AND RESCUE

When pilots were shot down—or when ground troops were separated from their units—helicopters were sent to find and rescue them. They carried 250-foot cables so they could pull troops out of thick jungles.

MOVING EQUIPMENT

Big helicopters carried artillery guns and other heavy equipment to distant combat zones. The largest choppers could airlift damaged helicopters.

The UH-1 Huey was the workhorse of the war.

Battle-weary American soldiers rest on the blasted slopes of Hamburger Hill.

everywhere. The place smelled like human waste. We walked silently past soldiers who'd been fighting for days. They looked like zombies. They were filthy and unshaven. And they had a glassy look in their eyes.

We called it the "thousand-mile stare"—the dead, distant gaze of men who spent too long in combat.

One soldier was looking at me with wide, wild eyes. "None of you will ever see the top of that hill!" he screamed like a crazy man. "You know why they call it Hamburger Hill? Because everyone who goes up there gets chewed up! I got friends lying up there and we can't even bring their bodies back down!"

Then he collapsed in tears.

MILITARY SPEAK

How many *platoons* in a *company*? This chart shows how **U.S.** military units are generally organized.

The shoulder patch of the 101st Airborne Division, also known as the "Screaming Eagles."

UNIT	LEADER	SIZE	FYI
SQUAD	sergeant	4–10 soldiers (also called troops)	A squad is the smallest fighting unit in the army.
PLATOON	lieutenant	about 16–40 soldiers (3–4 squads)	Platoons include riflemen, machine gunners, radio operators, and other specialists.
COMPANY	captain	100–200 soldiers (3–4 platoons)	The size of a company depends on its mission.
BATTALION	lieutenant colonel	500–1,000 soldiers (3–5 companies)	A battalion is capable of undertaking an independent combat mission.
BRIGADE/ REGIMENT	colonel	3,000–5,000 soldiers (3 or more battalions)	Some brigades are led by a brigadier general.
DIVISION	major general	10,000–18,000 soldiers (3 brigades/ regiments)	A division is big enough to conduct a major military operation.

May 20: "So This Is How I'm Gonna Die"

On the final day of the battle, my battalion started up the hill.

In the morning, jets mercilessly pulverized Hamburger Hill with bombs. As we began our ascent, I thought the enemy had to be dead. Who could survive such an assault? We saw trees blown

Men in Wiknik's unit on patrol during a later mission

into logs and body parts in the mud. I walked standing straight up, thinking the heavy fighting was over.

Then I noticed something strange. Little brown bubbles popped up from the dirt at my feet. I bent down to take a closer look and then I realized—they weren't bubbles. They were bullets striking the ground!

I hit the dirt. Hurriedly, I crawled into a bomb crater with another soldier. I couldn't see where the bullets were coming from, but they landed all around me. Suddenly, I was sprayed with water. I looked over at the other soldier. He'd been shot in the leg and the bullet had pierced his canteen.

He screamed in pain. I covered his wound with my hand. "It's not that bad," I told him, but his leg was bleeding heavily. A medic jumped into our crater. I realized that three men were an easy target, so I crawled to another crater.

Looking up the hill, I saw muzzle flashes about 50 feet away. I couldn't make out a target, so I lifted my gun over my head and fired up the hill. The shooting stopped for a second. Cautiously, I stuck my head up to see if I'd hit anything.

Then I felt a blinding sensation in my eyes. I didn't realize it, but a bullet had hit the dirt in front of me and sprayed earth into my face. When I reached up to protect my stinging eyes, another

On the last day of the Battle of Hamburger Hill—May 20—American soldiers fire at an enemy bunker near the top of the mountain.

bullet slammed into my chest. It lifted me off my feet and threw me back into the crater.

I was shot! I remember thinking, "So this is how I'm gonna die—at the bottom of a mud pit in the middle of nowhere."

The pain seared through my chest. I thought I'd just fade away. But when I looked down, I didn't see any blood. The shot smacked right into the magazine [a metal ammunition container] strapped to my chest. The bullet had bounced off me.

Then I did something crazy. I was tired of lying in that mud puddle waiting to die. I jumped from the crater. I yelled back to my squad, "Follow me!" as I sprinted wildly up the hill. I sprayed gunfire everywhere. When I turned around, I was at the top of Hamburger Hill. And completely alone. No one had followed me.

An American soldier stays low as he advances toward an enemy position. The thick jungles of South Vietnam provided plenty of hiding places for fighters from the North Vietnamese Army and the Viet Cong.

On Top of the Hill

In my mad dash, I'd run headlong through the enemy lines.

As I looked back, I saw the other GIs battling what remained of the NVA forces. For the next half hour, I watched from the summit as our soldiers finally beat back the enemy.

I looked down at the main battlefield—where the 3/187th [Frank Boccia's battalion] was first hit ten days earlier. It covered nearly half a mile. The plant life was stripped away. There was no trail anymore, just a desolate ridge lined with a dozen body bags, each containing a slain GI. The dead NVA—and pieces of them—were scattered on either side of the ridge. We found patches on their uniforms that read, "KILL AMERICANS."

The top of the hill was gray and gloomy. It looked like a lunar landscape. The mountain was now an anthill of soldiers. The stench of decaying flesh, the shriveled corpses, the silent body

Soldiers in the A Shau Valley wait for a MedEvac helicopter to land. The purple smoke flares were guiding the helicopter to a cleared landing zone.

bags, and the massive destruction would be my lasting memory of that hellish hill.

We cleaned up the summit and retrieved our dead. I saw a sign scrawled on a piece of cardboard. A GI had nailed it to a tree. It said "HAMBURGER HILL." As I watched, a weary soldier trudged to the sign and added a note at the bottom.

It read: "Was it worth it?"

HOME FROM THE WAR

FRANK BOCCIA

reached the top of Hamburger Hill on the last day of the battle. His battalion, the first unit on the hill, suffered staggering casualties—39 killed and 290 wounded. "The feeling among my men was blankness. We were numb," Boccia recalls. "We didn't celebrate. We had no sense of victory."

In December 1969, Boccia went home to his newborn son. Today he lives in Illinois. He has three kids and three grand-children. He doesn't talk much about Hamburger Hill. But every spring, he attends a reunion of soldiers from his battalion.

"I think back on how young we were," Frank says. "We thought we were invincible."

MIKE SERRANO

MIKE SERRANO was airlifted off the hill. He underwent several surgeries but still has shrapnel in his arm and legs.

He returned home in November 1969. But he couldn't leave thoughts of the hill behind. He was angry and depressed until he met the woman who would become his wife. "She was the first person who ever asked me, 'What happened to you over there?'" he recalls. "I broke down crying. I told her the whole story."

Serrano was haunted by Roger Pedue's death. After 20 years, he tracked down Pedue's brother in Indiana. Serrano told him that Roger died a hero. And Serrano asked for forgiveness. "I lived with guilt for so long," he says. "Finally I could start healing." Today, Serrano lives in West Sacramento, California, and helps veterans transition back into civilian life.

ARTHUR WIKNIK

ARTHUR WIKNIK served in Vietnam for another ten months after the Battle of Hamburger Hill. And he always carried the ammunition magazine that blocked the bullet and saved his life. Wiknik came home in 1970. His job and his Camaro were waiting for him, but his girlfriend dumped him.

Today, Wiknik is married and has three grown children. He is proud of his service to his country. "A lot of people don't want to talk about Vietnam, but not me," he says. Wiknik tells the story of Hamburger Hill to school classes and veterans groups. The license plates on his car and truck read "HAMHIL."

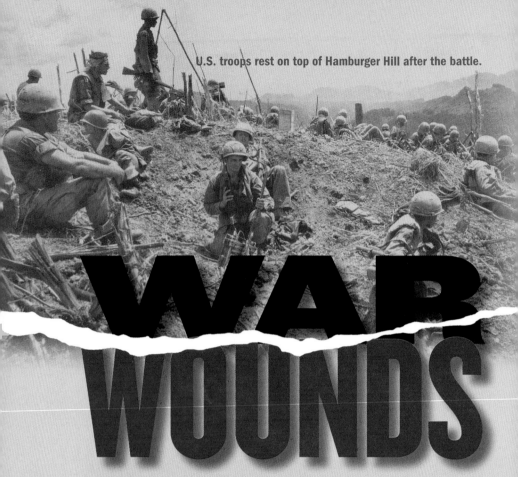

U.S. troops rest on top of Hamburger Hill after the battle.

WAR
WOUNDS

On May 20, 1969, U.S. soldiers finally reached the top of Hamburger Hill, and the surviving NVA troops retreated. But the victory was short-lived. Less than a month later, U.S. troops abandoned the hill. The goal of the assault had been to kill enemy soldiers, not seize territory. Within days, new NVA forces moved in.

After Hamburger Hill, there was little doubt that Americans had run out of patience with the Vietnam War. They wanted it over—as soon as possible.

South Vietnamese
troops training

In November 1969, President Richard Nixon began a policy he called "Vietnamization"—aggressively training the South Vietnamese army to prepare for a U.S. withdrawal.

But even as Nixon pulled troops out of Vietnam, he also spread the war. The U.S. conducted secret bombing missions over Laos and Cambodia. The two nations west of Vietnam were neutral. But the North set up bases and hid guns and supplies in their territory.

News of this "secret war" leaked out and sparked intense anti-war protests. With unrest at home and morale fading among the GIs, peace talks began in 1969. U.S. troops began to come home.

The War Ends

On January 27, 1973, all sides agreed to a cease-fire. The last U.S. troops flew out of Vietnam on March 29, 1973. They left behind a weakened South Vietnam, and by 1974, its government had collapsed. On April 30, 1975, NVA troops overran Saigon, the capital of South Vietnam. That same day, the country surrendered to the North.

The Vietnam War was over. Nearly 60,000 U.S. soldiers—and more than three million Vietnamese—had been killed. The United States had lost its first war. Many Americans had lost faith in their leaders. And the men and women who had served in Vietnam were often treated with scorn. They did not get the respect shown to veterans of other wars. It would take decades for the nation to heal from the wounds of Vietnam.

A visitor to the Vietnam Veterans Memorial in Washington, D.C., touches the name of one of the 58,261 dead or missing soldiers listed on the wall.

TIMELINE

1954: France withdraws from Vietnam after 100 years of colonization, and the nation is split in two. North Vietnam establishes a communist government, while South Vietnam is non-communist.

1961: To aid the South against communist attacks, the U.S. increases its military and economic support. By 1963, 16,000 American military advisers are in Vietnam.

1964: In response to alleged attacks on U.S. destroyers by North Vietnamese warships, Congress approves President Johnson's request to use armed forces to help South Vietnam.

1965: More than 200,000 U.S. troops are fighting in Vietnam. They're supported by massive aerial bombing.

1968: The North Vietnamese Army (NVA) and the Viet Cong launch the Tet Offensive, attacking cities and villages throughout South Vietnam.

1968: U.S. soldiers kill 500 civilians in the town of My Lai, a massacre that shocks the American public.

1969: With many Americans now against the war, President Richard Nixon promises to bring "peace with honor" to Vietnam.

1969: 1,800 U.S. troops battle to capture Hamburger Hill. Within weeks, they abandon the hill, and the NVA re-establishes control of the area.

1970: During an anti-war protest at Kent State University in Ohio, National Guardsmen fire into a crowd of protesters. Four students are killed.

1972: With American troops leaving, the North Vietnamese attack a weakened South Vietnam in the Easter Offensive.

1973: The Paris Peace Accords produce a cease-fire. Two months later, the last U.S. troops withdraw from Vietnam.

1975: North Vietnamese troops overrun Saigon, the capital of South Vietnam. The South surrenders, ending the war. Months later, Vietnam unifies as a communist country, the Socialist Republic of Vietnam.

RESOURCES

BOOKS

Caputo, Philip. *10,000 Days of Thunder: A History of the Vietnam War.* New York: Atheneum Books for Young Readers, 2005.

Gerdes, Louise I., ed. *The Vietnam War (Examining Issues Through Political Cartoons).* Farmington Hills, MI: Greenhaven Press, 2004.

Levy, Debbie. *The Vietnam War (Chronicle of America's Wars).* Minneapolis: Lerner Publications, 2004.

Mason, Andrew. *The Vietnam War: A Primary Source History (In Their Own Words).* Milwaukee: Gareth Stevens Publishing, 2006.

Murray, Stuart. *Vietnam War (DK Eyewitness Books).* New York: DK Publishing, 2005.

O'Connell, Kim A. *Primary Source Accounts of the Vietnam War (America's Wars Through Primary Sources).* Berkeley Heights, NJ: Enslow Publishers, 2006.

Schynert, Mark. *Women of the Vietnam War (Women in History).* Detroit: Lucent Books, 2005.

Smith-Llera, Danielle. *Vietnam War POWs (We the People).* Minneapolis: Compass Point Books, 2008.

WEBSITES

Vietnam Online
www.pbs.org/wgbh/amex/vietnam

The online companion to the PBS series *Vietnam: A Television History.*

Re: Vietnam: Stories Since the War
www.pbs.org/pov/stories

This site features personal stories about the Vietnam War and its impact.

Battlefield: Vietnam
www.pbs.org/battlefieldvietnam

This site includes a concise overview of the war and its causes.

The Virtual Wall
www.thevirtualwall.org

On this site, veterans, families, and friends can post remembrances of those who lost their lives during the Vietnam War.

Vietnam Magazine
www.historynet.com/magazines/vietnam

This is the website of *Vietnam,* a magazine about the war that features articles by military historians and firsthand accounts by veterans.

DICTIONARY

A

artillery (ar-TIL-uh-ree) *noun* large, powerful guns, usually mounted on wheels or tracks

C

canopy (KAN-uh-pee) *noun* the highest layer of a forest, formed by the tops of the tallest trees

communist (KOM-yuh-nist) *adjective* describing a system in which a one-party government controls the economic and political lives of a nation's citizens

D

demilitarized zone (DMZ) (dee-MIL-ih-tur-ized ZONE) *noun* during war, a neutral area where military activity is not permitted

draft (DRAFT) *noun* a system for selecting individuals for required military service

G

GI (jee-EYE) *noun* slang for an American soldier

grenade (gruh-NADE) *noun* a small bomb thrown by hand or fired from a rifle

guerrilla (guh-RIL-uh) *adjective* describing a type of warfare in which small groups of rebel fighters launch surprise attacks against an official army

I

infantry (IN-fuhn-tree) *noun* the part of an army that fights on foot

L

landing zone (LZ) (LAND-ing ZOHN) *noun* a military term for an area where helicopters or other aircraft land

M

magazine (MAG-uh-zeen) *noun* a container that holds bullets and feeds them into the gun

malevolent (muh-LEH-vuh-lint) *adjective* having or indicating a wish to do evil to others

MedEvac (MED-ih-vack) *noun* a helicopter used for emergency evacuation of the wounded from a combat area

mortar (MOR-tur) *noun* a very short cannon that fires shells or rockets high in the air

muzzle flash (MUHZ-uhl FLASH) *noun* the burst of light that can be seen when a firearm goes off

N

napalm (NAY-palm) *noun* a highly flammable jelly used in firebombs and flamethrowers

North Vietnamese Army (NVA) (NORTH vee-et-nuh-MEEZ ARM-ee) *noun* the armed forces of communist-led North Vietnam

P

pulverize (PUHL-vuh-rahyz) *verb* to destroy completely

R

reconnaissance mission (ruh-CON-uh-sinss MISH-uhn) *noun* exploration of an area to gain information about enemy activity

rocket-propelled grenade (RPG) (ROK-it pruh-PELD gruh-NADE) *noun* a hand-held, shoulder-launched weapon that fires grenades; meant to be aimed at vehicles or bunkers

S

shrapnel (SHRAP-nuhl) *noun* small pieces of metal scattered by an exploding shell or bomb

spider hole (SPYE-dur HOLE) *noun* a small, well-hidden, one-person foxhole

V

Viet Cong (vee-ET KONG) *noun* communist rebels in South Vietnam who were allied with the North Vietnamese Army during the Vietnam War

INDEX

81-mm mortar, 21
101st Airborne Division, 16, 30,
  38, 49
187th Regiment, 16, 17, 31, 52
506th Infantry Regiment, 30,
  31, 44

airborne assault helicopters, 47
AK-47 assault rifles, 19, 21
ambush, 11, 23, 34, 35, 37
ammunition, 20, 34, 45, 46
A Shau Valley, 1, 12, 17, **19**, **31**,
  45, **53**

battalions, 16, 17, 30, 31, 44,
  49, 50, 52, 54
Boccia, Frank, **16**, 17–19, 22–
  24, 26–27, 30, 31, 52, **54**
bombing missions, 18, 45, 50,
  57, 58
brigades, 49
bunkers, 24, 34, 46

calendar, **37**
Cambodia, **6**, **19**, 57
canteen, **22**
Carter, Jimmy, 33
casualties, 12, 34, 35, 38–39,
  47, 50, 51, 52, 53, 54, 57
cease-fire, 57, 58
CH-47 Chinook helicopter, 47
China Beach, 31
communism, 9, 10, 58
companies, 23, 24, 37, 45,
  46, 49

Da Nang, **8**
democracy, 10
divisions, 16, 30, 44, 49

dog tag, **46**
door gunners, 46, 47
Dong Ap Bia, 3
draft, **9**, 30, **33**, 44

Eagle Beach, 45
Easter Offensive, 58

grenades, 19, 20, 21, 22, 24,
  27, **38**, 45, 47

Hamburger Hill, **2–3**, **6**, 13,
  14–15, 16, 30, 34, **42–43**,
  44, **45**, 46, 48, 49, 50, **51**,
  52, 53, 54, 55, **56**
helicopters, 17, **18**, 34, 39, 41,
  45, 46, **47**
Ho Chi Minh, 9, 10
Ho Chi Minh Trail, **19**
Honeycutt, Weldon, 16, 17,
  24, 27

Johnson, Lyndon, 10, 58

Killing Zone, 24, 26

Laos, **6**, **19**, 57
"lifers," 32, 34

M-16 rifles, 20, 38, 46
M-60 machine gun, **20**, 46
M-79 "Thumper" grenade
  launcher, 20
Mark 2 grenade, 20
MedEvac helicopters, 28, 39,
  40–41, 47, **53**
medics, **14**, 38, 39, 41, 50
mouth-to-mouth resuscitation,
  38

My Lai massacre, 58

napalm, **18**, 45
Ngo Dinh Diem, 9, 10
Nixon, Richard, 57, 58
North Vietnam, **6**, 9, 10, 12,
    19, 58
North Vietnamese Army (NVA),
    11, 13, **17**, 22, 24, 26, 31,
    34–35, 38, 46, 52, 56,
    57, 58

Operation Apache Snow, 13

Paige, Chuck, 31
Paris Peace Accords, 57, 58
Pedue, Roger, **32**, 34, 35, 37,
    38, 39, 41, 55
platoons, 17, 18, 31, 32, 35, 49
point man, 35, **36**, 37
protests, 12, **13**, **33**, 57, 58

radio operators, **35**, 37, 39
regiments, 16, 24, 30, 44, 49
retreat, 13, 26, 27, 56
rocket-propelled grenades
    (RPGs), 19, **21**, 22, 24

Serrano, Mike, **1**, 3, 13, **30**, **31**,
    32, 34, 35, 36–39, 41, 55
shrapnel, 20, 38, 39, 55
Snyder, John, **26**, 27
Socialist Republic of Vietnam,
    58
South Vietnam, **6**, 9, 10, 12, **19**,
    57, 58
spider holes, 9, **24**, 38
squads, 35, 49
Stone, Oliver, 11

Tet Offensive, **12**, 58
Thailand, **6**, **19**
"thousand mile stare," 48
timeline, 58
transport helicopters, **47**

UH-1 Huey helicopters, 17, **47**

Viet Cong rebels, 10, **11**, **37**,
    52, 58
"Vietnamization," 57
Vietnam Veterans Memorial, **57**

Westman, Miles, **26**
Wiknik, Arthur, 43, **44**, 45, 46,
    48, 50–51, 52–53, **55**
World War II, 17, 30, 47

ABOUT THIS BOOK

While researching this book, I talked to about a dozen Hamburger Hill veterans. Most of them had very different experiences. And none of them said they regret going to Vietnam. But almost all agreed on one thing:

Vietnam changed them.

Mike Serrano told me that when he returned home from Vietnam, he just couldn't fit back into his old life. He didn't feel normal. I asked him when he finally felt better. He replied, "I still don't."

Whether they believed the war was justified or not, the veterans I talked to described combat as horrific. All they thought about was keeping themselves and their friends alive—and getting back home.

But home had changed too. While veterans of other wars came back to parades, Vietnam vets were sometimes treated with scorn and abuse. Americans were angered by the war—and often blamed the soldiers.

When Arthur Wiknik came back from Vietnam in 1970, he proudly strolled through an airport in his medal-laden uniform. "I was on top of the world," he remembers. He expected to be congratulated for his service. Instead, harsh glares and taunts surrounded him. "I felt like running and hiding," he says. "I wanted to take that uniform off as fast as I could."

Today's veterans generally have a different kind of homecoming. Their sacrifices are more often understood and appreciated. For Mike, that's a welcome change. He works with returning soldiers to help them fit back into civilian life. "In a lot of ways, when I look at them, I see myself," he says. "The big difference is that when they come home, there's somebody here to help them. It's something we never had."

Most of the information in this book came from interviews with Vietnam veterans. Here are some other sources that were critical to my research:

Caputo, Philip. *10,000 Days of Thunder: A History of the Vietnam War.* New York: Atheneum Books For Younger Readers, 2005.

Gilmore, Donald L. with D. M. Giangreco. *Eyewitness Vietnam: Firsthand Accounts From Operation Rolling Thunder to the Fall of Saigon.* New York: Sterling Publishing Company, 2006.

Wiknik, Arthur Jr. *Nam Sense: Surviving Vietnam with the 101st Airborne Division.* Havertown, PA: Casemate, 2005.

Zaffiri, Samuel. *Hamburger Hill.* Novato, CA: Presidio Press Inc., 1988.

—John DiConsiglio